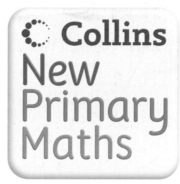

Collins New Primary Maths

Pupil Book 3C

Series Editor: Peter Clarke

Authors: Jeanette Mumford, Sandra Roberts, Andrew Edmondson

Contents

Page number

Rounding weights

● **Round numbers to the nearest 10 or 100**

How much do each of these objects weigh? Write your answer to the nearest 100 g.

a 
584 g

b 
450 g

c 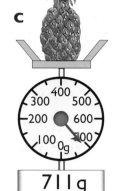
711 g

Example

233 g rounded to the nearest 100 g is 200 g.

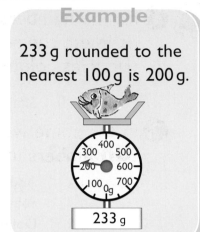

233 g

1 Round these weights to the nearest 100 g.

a  179 g

b  784 g

c 64 g

d 350 g

e 42 g

2 Round these weights to the nearest 100 kg and to the nearest 10 kg.

a 235 kg

b  763 kg

c 72 kg

d 350 kg

e 125 kg

3 These weights are to the nearest 100 g. Write the lightest and heaviest possible weights for each animal.

a  400 g

b  300 g

c  700 g

d 100 g

a Use the following digits to make six different 3-digit numbers.

b Then round each number

  i to the nearest 10

  ii to the nearest 100.

4

Star estimates

● **Use rounding to estimate a sum or difference**

1 Round numbers to the nearest 10 and estimate the sum of the numbers in the triangles coloured:

a blue   **b** red   **c** green

2 In the same way find the difference between the numbers in the triangles coloured:

a white   **b** yellow

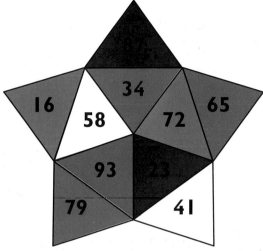

1 Round numbers to the nearest 10 and estimate the sum of the numbers in the triangles coloured:

a blue   **b** red   **c** green
d white   **e** purple **f** yellow

2 Round numbers to the nearest 10 and estimate the difference between these numbers on the star.

a two highest numbers

b two lowest numbers

c highest and lowest even numbers

d highest and lowest odd numbers

Example

16 → 20/72 → 70

20 + 70 → 90

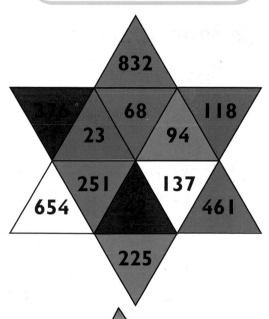

1 Round the numbers on each star to the nearest 100. Show that you can make 3 different addition sums.

2 Round the numbers on each star to the nearest 10. Show that you can make 3 different subtraction sums.

Add it up

● **Develop and use written methods for addition**

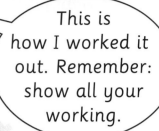

31 + 16 =

30 + 1 + 10 + 6

30 + 10 + 6 + 1 = 47

 ❶ Work out these addition calculations.

a 23 + 5 = ☐   b 3 + 24 = ☐

c 41 + 5 = ☐   d 27 + 8 = ☐

e 53 + 8 = ☐   f 68 + 6 = ☐

g 41 + 37 = ☐   h 46 + 23 = ☐

i 52 + 24 = ☐   j 63 + 27 = ☐

k 31 + 57 = ☐   l 42 + 35 = ☐

m 74 + 55 = ☐   n 86 + 39 = ☐

o 65 + 72 = ☐   p 79 + 46 = ☐

This is how I worked it out. Remember: show all your working.

❷ Explain why you chose the method you used.

 ❶ Add the numbers showing your working.

a 47 + 75 = ☐   b 86 + 34 = ☐

c 75 + 92 = ☐   d 167 + 31 = ☐

e 155 + 68 = ☐   f 297 + 85 = ☐

g 81 + 269 = ☐   h 78 + 164 = ☐

i 267 + 94 = ☐   j 62 + 243 = ☐

k 91 + 187 = ☐   l 241 + 165 = ☐

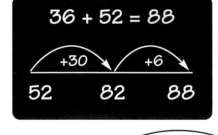

36 + 52 = 88

+30   +6

52   82   88

I think I'll use the empty number line.

❷ Explain why you chose the method you used.

Write two tips to help someone with addition of pairs of two-digit or three-digit numbers.

Subtract it

● **Develop and use written methods for subtraction**

Work with your partner. Both work out a calculation and then explain your methods to each other.

a 46 − 5 = ☐   b 38 − 5 = ☐   c 55 − 9 = ☐

d 67 − 43 = ☐   e 74 − 42 = ☐   f 87 − 54 = ☐

g 65 − 37 = ☐   h 48 − 29 = ☐   i 72 − 35 = ☐

j 94 − 46 = ☐   k 75 − 27 = ☐   l 47 − 18 = ☐

m 53 − 39 = ☐   n 91 − 35 = ☐   o 82 − 43 = ☐

1 a 92 − 46 = ☐   b 73 − 35 = ☐   c 64 − 28 = ☐

d 149 − 27 = ☐   e 156 − 38 = ☐   f 174 − 45 = ☐

g 181 − 39 = ☐   h 163 − 27 = ☐   i 126 − 44 = ☐

j 145 − 53 = ☐   k 138 − 46 = ☐   l 162 − 84 = ☐

m 151 − 93 = ☐   n 139 − 62 = ☐   o 176 − 89 = ☐

2 Look at the picture. What is the same about the two methods the children have used?

Write two tips to help someone with subtraction.

Picnic time

● **Solve one-step and two-step word problems**

Pink class is going on a picnic. Here are their sandwiches.

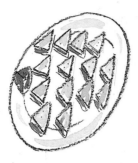    

14 cheese   21 ham   16 salad   40 jam   9 egg

Answer the questions. Remember to show your working.

1 How many ham and egg sandwiches are there altogether?

2 How many jam and cheese sandwiches are there in total?

3 Only nine of the salad sandwiches are eaten. How many are left?

4 Next time Pink class go on a picnic they want double the number of cheese sandwiches. How many will that be?

5 Six of the ham sandwiches got squashed. How many were left?

1 How many sandwiches are there altogether?

2 All the egg sandwiches get left on the bus. How many sandwiches are there at the picnic?

3 If all the salad and cheese sandwiches are eaten, how many sandwiches are left?

4 If all the ham and jam sandwiches are eaten, how many sandwiches are left?

5 If next time the class have double the number of ham sandwiches and the same number of all the others, what will be the total number of sandwiches?

If next time the class have three times the amount of sandwiches, how many will that be?

Reviewing multiplication and division facts (1)

● Know multiplication facts for the 2, 3, 4, 5, 6 and 10 times tables and the related division facts

Choose a flower and a pot to make a multiplication calculation.
Write the answer.
Your teacher will tell you how many calculations to make.

Divide each of the:

– roses by 2, 4 and 8

– sunflowers by 3 and 6

– daffodils by 5 and 10.

Example

$8 \div 2 = 4$

$8 \div 4 = 2$

$8 \div 8 = 1$

| 0 | 1 | 2 | 3 | 4 | 5 | 6 | 7 | 8 | 9 | × | = |

Investigate how many different multiplication calculations you can make using the digit cards.

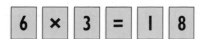 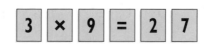

You need:

● set of 0–9 digit cards

● multiplication symbol card

● equals symbol card

Reviewing multiplication and division facts (2)

● Know by heart the multiplication facts for the 2, 3, 4, 5, 6 and 10 times tables and the related division facts

1 Copy and complete the table.

×	3	8	6	5	7	9	10	4
2	6							
10								
5								

2 Copy and complete.

a $70 \div 10 = \square$ b $20 \div 2 = \square$ c $30 \div 3 = \square$ d $25 \div 5 = \square$

e $20 \div 4 = \square$ f $15 \div 3 = \square$ g $45 \div 5 = \square$ h $80 \div 10 = \square$

i $12 \div 2 = \square$ j $30 \div 10 = \square$ k $16 \div 2 = \square$ l $45 \div 9 = \square$

3 Copy and complete.

a $2 \times \square = 8$ b $10 \times \square = 90$ c $6 \div \square = 3$ d $\square \div 8 = 2$

e $30 \div \square = 6$ f $\square \div 2 = 10$ g $\square \times 4 = 20$ h $7 \times \square = 35$

1 Copy and complete the table.

×	8	9	3	4	6	7	10	5
6	48							
4								
3								

2 Copy and complete.

a $21 \div 3 =$ b $12 \div 6 =$ c $15 \div 3 =$ d $42 \div 7 =$

e $16 \div 4 =$ f $36 \div 9 =$ g $36 \div 6 =$ h $27 \div 9 =$

i $48 \div 8 =$ j $28 \div 4 =$ k $80 \div 8 =$ l $50 \div 10 =$

3 Copy and complete.

a $\square \times 8 = 16$ b $6 \times \square = 42$ c $\square \div 4 = 4$ d $48 \div \square = 6$

e $24 \div \square = 8$ f $\square \div 9 = 4$ g $9 \times \square = 45$ h $7 \times \square = 28$

Use the clues to find the numbers.

a Multiply me by 8 and the answer is 48.

b I am the eighth multiple of 5.

c I am a multiple of 6 between 35 and 40.

d I am the only two-digit multiple of 6 with 2 tens.

e I am a multiple of 4. I am less than 50. I have the same tens and units digit.

f There are 4 of us. Each one of us is a multiple of 5 and 10. We are all less than 50.

g I am the result of multiplying 3 and 7.

h When I am multiplied by myself the answer is 16.

Multiplying larger numbers

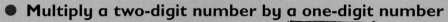

● **Multiply a two-digit number by a one-digit number**

1 Buy 3 tickets. How much money will you need?
Write a multiplication number sentence for each of the following.

a 20p   b 13p   c 40p   d 18p   e 15p

2 Buy 4 tickets. How much money will you need?
Write a multiplication number sentence for each of the following.

a 12p   b 20p   c 30p   d 17p   e 19p

How much money will you need?
Write a multiplication number sentence for each of the following.

1 a Buy 3 tickets. **2 a** Buy 6 tickets. **3 a** Buy 3 tickets. **4 a** Buy 4 tickets.

b Buy 5 tickets. **b** Buy 9 tickets. **b** Buy 8 tickets. **b** Buy 6 tickets.

Raffle

23p

Bouncy castle

24p

Show

32p

Tombola

47p

Roll the dice and write down the number.

Roll the dice again and multiply the previous number by the new dice number.

Roll the dice again and multiply the previous number by the new dice number.

How far can you go?

Example

6

$6 \times 8 = 48$

$48 \times 5 = 240$

$240 \times$

You need:
● 0–9 dice

Dividing two-digit numbers

● Divide a two-digit number by a one-digit number

Example

$98 ÷ 6 = (60 + 38) ÷ 6$
$= (60 ÷ 6) + (38 ÷ 6)$
$= 10 + 6 \text{ R2}$
$= 16 \text{ R2}$

$97 ÷ 4 = (80 + 17) ÷ 4$
$= (80 ÷ 4) + (17 ÷ 4)$
$= 20 + 4 \text{ R1}$
$= 24 \text{ R1}$

● Choose one number from each team to make a division calculation.
● Approximate the answer first and write it down.
● Then work out the answer.
● Your teacher will tell you how many different division calculations to make.

Solving word problems

● **Solve word problems involving 'real life' and money**

Answer these as quickly as you can.

a 2 × 6 = ☐   **b** 30 × 3 = ☐   **c** 42 ÷ 6 = ☐

d 3 × 4 = ☐   **e** 4 × 40 = ☐   **f** 32 ÷ 4 = ☐

g 4 × 9 = ☐   **h** 5 × 20 = ☐   **i** 40 ÷ 5 = ☐

j 5 × 7 = ☐   **k** 2 × 15 = ☐   **l** 800 ÷ 10 = ☐

m 10 × 10 = ☐   **n** 3 × 32 = ☐   **o** 600 ÷ 100 = ☐

p 40 × 5 = ☐   **q** 4 × 21 = ☐   **r** 900 ÷ 10 = ☐

Read each word problem. Work out the answer.

Remember

Show all your working

a There are 23 cakes in each box. Sue buys three boxes. How many cakes are there altogether?

b There are 24 children in one class. One day a third of them wore blue shirts. How many children was this?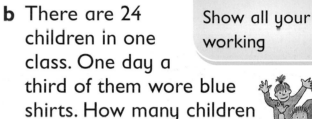

c There are 72 rocks in three boxes. The same number of rocks are in each box. How many rocks are there in each box?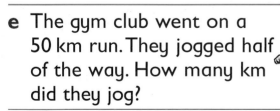

d The P.E. cupboard has 240 balls. Half of them are flat. How many are not flat?

e The gym club went on a 50 km run. They jogged half of the way. How many km did they jog?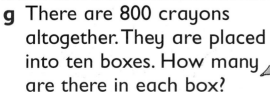

f Footballs cost £6 each. Hope Primary School buys 38. How much do they spend?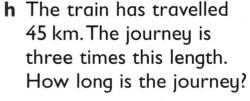

g There are 800 crayons altogether. They are placed into ten boxes. How many are there in each box?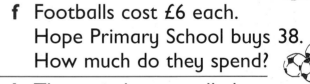

h The train has travelled 45 km. The journey is three times this length. How long is the journey?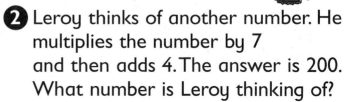

 1 Leroy thinks of a number. He divides the number by 4 and then subtracts 4. The answer is 15. What number is Leroy thinking of?

2 Leroy thinks of another number. He multiplies the number by 7 and then adds 4. The answer is 200. What number is Leroy thinking of?

Plasticine fractions

- Identify fractions of shapes

Write the fraction that each plasticine shape has been divided into. Write what fraction of each shape is orange and what fraction is blue.

a 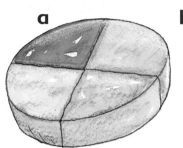 **b**  **c**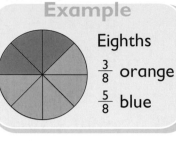

Example
Eighths
$\frac{3}{8}$ orange
$\frac{5}{8}$ blue
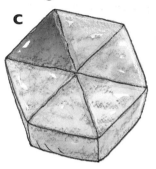

d 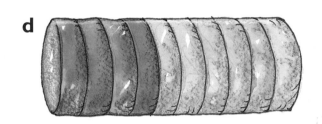 **e**

1 Write what fraction of each plasticine block has been squashed. The two fractions will total a whole.

2 Explain how you know that the sum of the two fractions are the same as a whole.

a  $\frac{1}{2}$ **b** 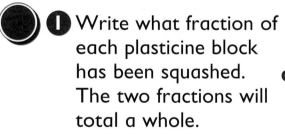 $\frac{4}{5}$ **c**  $\frac{2}{3}$

d  $\frac{1}{4}$ **e** 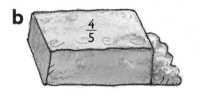 $\frac{2}{5}$ **f** 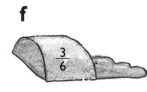 $\frac{3}{6}$

Write the fractions of each plasticine block that have been squashed. Each block must total one.

a $\frac{2}{5}$ $\frac{1}{5}$

b $\frac{3}{10}$ $\frac{2}{10}$ $\frac{3}{10}$

c $\frac{2}{10}$ $\frac{4}{10}$

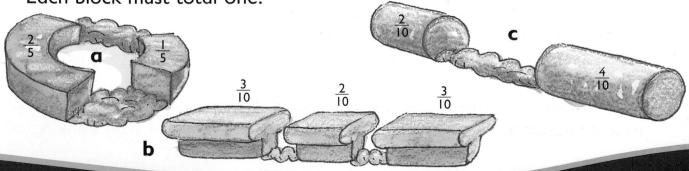

Making halves

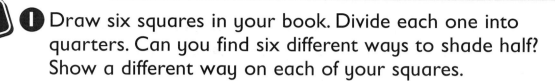
● **Use diagrams to compare fractions and show equivalents**

1 Draw six squares in your book. Divide each one into quarters. Can you find six different ways to shade half? Show a different way on each of your squares.

2 What fraction of each square have you shaded? Can you write it in two ways?

1 Draw six rectangles in your book. Divide each one into quarters. Can you find six different ways to shade half? Show a different way on each of your rectangles.

2 What fraction of each rectangle have you shaded? Can you write it in two ways?

 Explain why $\frac{1}{2}$, $\frac{2}{4}$ and $\frac{3}{6}$ are the same. Use diagrams to illustrate your explanation.

Continue the pattern

● **Identify patterns of numbers**

Use the patterns to help you work out the answers.

a
4 + 2 = ☐
4 + 12 = ☐
4 + 22 = ☐
4 + 32 = ☐

b
6 + 2 = ☐
6 + 12 = ☐
6 + 22 = ☐
6 + 32 = ☐

c
4 + 3 = ☐
4 + 13 = ☐
4 + 23 = ☐
4 + 33 = ☐

d
38 – 5 = ☐
38 – 15 = ☐
38 – 25 = ☐

e
34 – 3 = ☐
34 – 13 = ☐

f
1 + 5 = ☐
10 + 50 = ☐
100 + 500 = ☐

● Use the patterns to help you work out the answers.

a
76 – 4 = ☐
76 – 14 = ☐
76 – 24 = ☐
76 – 34 = ☐
76 – 54 = ☐
76 – 64 = ☐

b
15 + 4 = ☐
15 + 14 = ☐
15 + 24 = ☐
15 + 34 = ☐
15 + 64 = ☐
15 + 84 = ☐

c
12 + 5 = ☐
12 + 15 = ☐
12 + 25 = ☐
12 + 35 = ☐
12 + 55 = ☐
12 + 75 = ☐

d
97 – 3 = ☐
97 – 13 = ☐
97 – 23 = ☐
97 – 33 = ☐
97 – 43 = ☐
97 – 53 = ☐

e
89 – 5 = ☐
89 – 15 = ☐
89 – 25 = ☐
89 – 35 = ☐
89 – 65 = ☐
89 – 75 = ☐

f
8 + 7 = ☐
80 + 70 = ☐
800 + 700 = ☐

❶ Write a 2-digit + 1-digit calculation and continue the pattern. How far can you go?

❷ Write a 2-digit – 1-digit calculation and continue the pattern. How far can you go?

Magic squares

● In a puzzle find numbers that match a property

In this square of numbers, the sum of each row, column and diagonal is the same. It is called a magic square. The magic number in this magic square is 18.

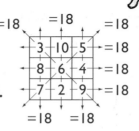

Example

8	4	7

8 + 4 + 7 = 19

① Find the total of each of these rows.

a
7	3	5

b
9	3	7

c
5	4	6

d
2	8	7

e
6	6	5

f
10	11	5

② Find the missing number which will make each row add to match its total.

a Total = 19
7	?	4

b Total = 20
5	8	?

c Total = 21
9	6	?

Copy and complete these squares to make them magic!

a Magic number = ☐

4		
	5	
	1	6

b Magic number= ☐

11	7	3
		8

c Magic number = ☐

5		9
	8	
7		

d Magic number = 36

	12	16
		11

e Magic number = 42

		11
10		18

① Place the numbers 1, 2 and 3 in the 9 boxes of the grid so that the 3 numbers in each row and column total 6.

② Using the rule 'total of 6', find how many different ways you can arrange the numbers 1, 2 and 3 in the 9 boxes.

You need:

● copy of RCM: 3 × 3 square grids

Juggling with numbers

● **In a puzzle find numbers that match a property**

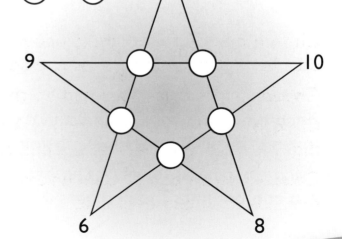

Use the numbers on the juggling balls to make these totals.

a ◯ + ◯ + ◯ = 9   **b** ◯ + ◯ + ◯ = 9

c ◯ + ◯ + ◯ = 10   **d** ◯ + ◯ + ◯ = 10

e ◯ + ◯ + ◯ = 11   **f** ◯ + ◯ + ◯ = 11

❶ Put the numbers 1 to 6 in the circles so that each side of the triangle totals the number shown in the box.

a

Total = 10

b

Total = 11

c

Total = 12

❷ Place the numbers 2, 3, 4, 5, 6 and 7 in the circles so that each side of the triangle is:

a a total of 12

b a total of 15.

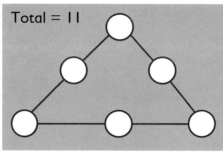

In this magic pentagon, each side totals 24. Copy the diagram and find the five missing numbers in the circles.

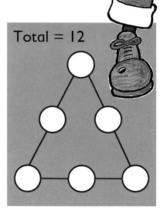

12

9   10

6   8

Number sequences

● **Recognise and continue number patterns**

Copy and continue each of the following number sequences.

1 6, 8, 10, 12, 14, ☐, ☐, ☐, ☐

2 15, 20, 25, 30, 35, 40, ☐, ☐, ☐, ☐

3 90, 80, 70, 60, 50, ☐, ☐, ☐, ☐

4 350, 355, 360, 365, ☐, ☐, ☐, ☐

5 740, 730, 720, 710, ☐, ☐, ☐, ☐

6 288, 290, 292, 294, ☐, ☐, ☐, ☐

7 586, 584, 582, 580, ☐, ☐, ☐, ☐

8 760, 755, 750, 745, ☐, ☐, ☐, ☐

1 Copy and complete each of the following number sequences.

a 9, 12, 15, 18, 21, ☐, ☐, ☐, ☐

b 24, 28, 32, 36, 40, ☐, ☐, ☐, ☐

c 24, 30, 36, 42, 48, ☐, ☐, ☐, ☐

d 95, 91, 87, 83, 79, ☐, ☐, ☐, ☐

e 85, 88, 91, 94, ☐, ☐, ☐, ☐

f 71, 65, 59, 53, ☐, ☐, ☐, ☐

g 425, 427, ☐, ☐, 433, ☐, ☐, 439

h 284, 279, ☐, 269, ☐, ☐, 254, ☐

i ☐, ☐, 355, ☐, 375, 385, 395, ☐

j ☐, 161, 165, ☐, 173, ☐, 181, ☐

2 Write 10 three-digit multiples of 2.

3 Write 10 three-digit multiples of 5.

4 Write 10 three-digit multiples of 10.

5 Write 10 three-digit multiples of 3.

3   8   15   26   45   72   84   92   100

1 Choose one of the numbers above. Write a sequence that has your number as its middle number.

2 Choose another number and do the same thing.

3 Choose any two numbers and write a sequence that has your numbers as the end two numbers.

4 Choose any three numbers and write a sequence that has your numbers in it.

Multiplication and division facts games

● **Know by heart the multiplication facts for the 2, 3, 4, 5, 6 and 10 times tables and the related division facts**

2 games to play in groups.

Spinner A

1	2	3	4	5	6
7	8	9	10	12	14
15	16	18	20	21	24
25	27	28	30	32	35
36	40	42	45	48	50
54	60	70	80	90	100

You need:
● paper clip
● pencil and paper

Spinner B

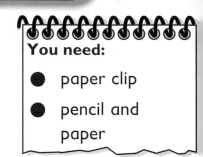

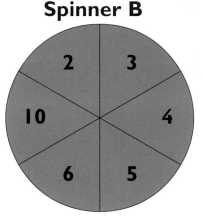

Each player writes down any 10 numbers from the grid.
Take turns to:
● spin both spinners
● multiply the two numbers together.
If the answer is one of your numbers, cross it out. If not, do nothing.
The winner is the first person to cross out all their numbers.

Each player writes down any 10 numbers from the grid.
Take turns to:
● spin spinner B, e.g. 6
● find one of your 10 numbers that is a multiple of the spinner number and say the related division calculation to the rest of the group, i.e. 18 divided by 6 equals 3.
If the answer is correct, cross out the number.
If the number has already been crossed out or you cannot find one of your numbers that is a multiple of the spinner number, do nothing.
The winner is the first person to cross out all their numbers.

Which numbers should you choose from the grid to give yourself the best chance of winning? Why would you choose these numbers?

Multiplying multiples of 10 and 100

● **Multiply one-digit numbers by multiples of 10 and 100**

Copy and complete.

a 7 x 3 = ◯   **b** 9 x 2 = ◯   **c** 4 x 10 = ◯

d 4 x 4 = ◯   **e** 8 x 6 = ◯   **f** 4 x 3 = ◯

g 6 x 6 = ◯   **h** 8 x 4 = ◯   **i** 8 x 2 = ◯

j 7 x 10 = ◯   **k** 9 x 5 = ◯   **l** 9 x 6 = ◯

m 3 x 5 = ◯   **n** 7 x 2 = ◯   **o** 8 x 5 = ◯

Multiply each of the bats by 4 and 6 and each of the ghosts by 3 and 5.

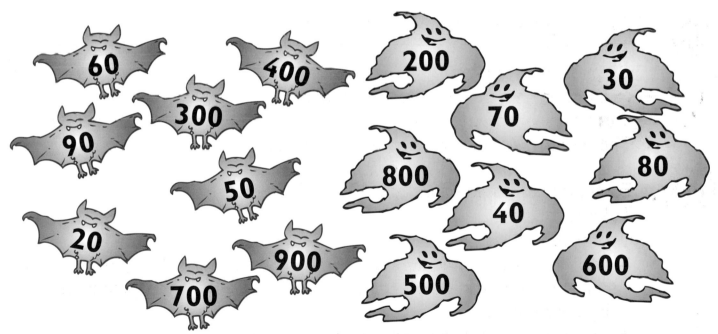

Choose four of the following cards to make a correct number sentence.

| 4 | 40 | 400 | 4000 | ×10 | ×100 | ÷10 | ÷100 | = |

● How many different number sentences can you make by arranging the cards?
● Write about what you notice.

Estimating and checking

● **Estimate and check calculations**

Example		
27 × 4 =		
Estimate	**Calculate**	**Check**
30 × 4 = 120	20 × 4 = 80	27 × 2 = 54
	7 × 4 = 28	54 × 2 = 108
	80 + 28 = 108	

Example		
73 ÷ 3 =		
Estimate	**Calculate**	**Check**
75 ÷ 3 = 25	(60 + 13) ÷ 3	24 × 3
	= (60 ÷ 3) + (13 ÷ 3)	20 × 3 = 60
	= 20 + 4 R1	4 × 3 = 12
	= 24 R1	60 + 12 + 1 = 73

1 Estimate the answer to each of these calculations. Show all your working.

a 14 × 8	b 23 × 4	c 17 × 5
d 72 ÷ 4	e 81 ÷ 3	f 94 ÷ 2

2 Work out the answer to each of the above calculations.
Show all your working.

3 Check your answer to each of the calculations above.
Show all your working.

1 Estimate the answer to each of these calculations. Show all your working.

a 39 × 6	b 73 × 4	c 54 × 8
d 98 ÷ 6	e 91 ÷ 4	f 87 ÷ 5

2 Work out the answer to each of the above calculations.
Show all your working.

3 Check your answer to each of the calculations above. Show all your
working.

1 Estimate the answer to each of these calculations. Show all your working.

a 56 × 7	b 64 × 9	c 62 × 8
d 86 ÷ 6	e 85 ÷ 3	f 79 ÷ 4

2 Work out the answer to each of the above calculations.
Show all your working.

3 Check your answer to each of the calculations above. Show all your working.

Which operation?

● **Solve word problems involving 'real life' and money**

`10 + 5`

For each of the word problems below, choose the correct operation card.

`9 + 3` `9 × 3`

`24 × 2` `24 ÷ 2` `9 ÷ 3`

a Balls are sold in packs of three. I buy nine balls altogether. How many packs did I buy?

b Joanne saved £10 in 5 weeks. How much did she save each week?

`10 × 5` `200 ÷ 10`

`50 − 10` `10 × 50` `10 ÷ 5`

c There are three bags of apples and nine apples in each bag. How many apples are there altogether?

d There are ten children with five pencils each. How many pencils are there?

e John works for 50 weeks a year. He gets paid £10 a week. How much money does he make in a year?

f There are 24 children. How many eyes do they have altogether?

Remember

Show all your working

1 Write the answer to each of the calculations in the section.

2 Read these word problems. Find the important information. Decide which operation you will use. First write the calculation. Then write the answer to the problem.

a Mum gave me 90p. She told me to give half to my brother. How much did we get each?

b I have £46. Tickets cost £5. How many can I buy?

c Balloons are sold in packs of 45. I buy 6 packs. How many balloons do I buy altogether?

d Mr Young has £700. A television costs £450. Does he have enough money to buy two televisions? If so, how much money does he have left? If not, how much more money does he need?

e Jim has £2. Hamburgers cost 65p each. Jim buys three. How much change does he get?

f The class of 28 children made teams to play basketball. There were five players on a team. How many more children do they need so everyone can play?

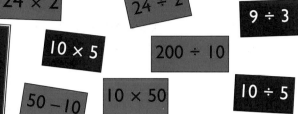

Choose three of the calculations in the section and write a word problem for each.

Building tetrominoid city

● **Build solid shapes to match pictures of them**

Use four cubes each time to build these tetrominoid houses.

a

b

c

d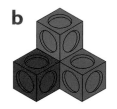

e

You need:

●●● interlocking cubes

 1 Use cubes to build these houses for tetrominoids.

a

b

c

d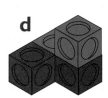

e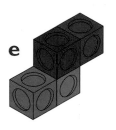

2 Some tetrominoids decided to add a one cube extension to their designs. Use your cubes to build these houses.

a

b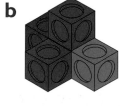

c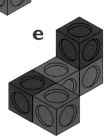

d

e

Now build your own houses. Using five cubes each time, build five different solid shapes.

Puzzling triangles

● Make shapes that match a property

1 a Join 2 triangles along matching edges to make these shapes.

You need:

● 3 right-angled isosceles triangles
● 1 cm square dot paper
● ruler

b Draw the 2 shapes on square dot paper. Show how the triangles fit together.

2 Join 3 triangles along matching edges to make a pentagon. Record as in 1b.

1 Work with a partner.

a Join 4 triangles along matching edges to make these shapes.

i  **ii**

You need:

● 8 right-angled isosceles triangles
● 1 cm squared dot paper
● ruler

iii

b Draw the 3 shapes on square dot paper. Show how the triangles fit together.

2 Join 6 triangles along matching edges to make these shapes. Record as in 1b.

a hexagon   **b** pentagon   **c** octagon

Sarah said: 'You can make at least 5 different quadrilaterals by joining 8 right-angled triangles.' True or false? Investigate.

Puzzling outlines

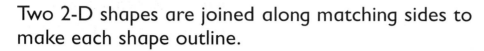

● Make shapes that match a property

You need:

● Regular 2-D shapes with matching sides

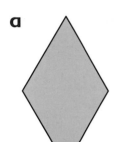

Two 2-D shapes are joined along matching sides to make each shape outline.

Name each shape outline.

a 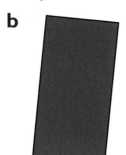 b 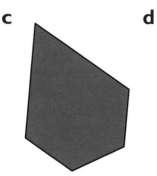 c  d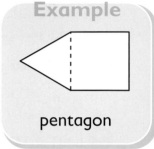

Example

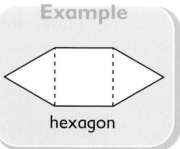

pentagon

 **1** Take two triangles and one regular shape. Fit them together to make these shapes. Name each shape.

a  b

Example

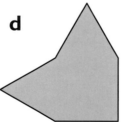

hexagon

c d

You need:

● set-square

●● Regular 2-D shapes with sides the same length

2 Solve these puzzles about the shape outlines in question **1**.

a I have 2 angles smaller than a right angle and 2 angles greater than a right angle. Which outline am I?

b I have 1 right angle and 3 angles more than a right angle. How many of my other angles are less than a right angle?

a Take 4 △ and 1 ▢. Fit them together to make a four-pointed star.

b Take 5 △ and 1 ⬠. Fit them together to make a five-pointed star.

c Take 6 △ and 1 ⬡. Fit them together to make a six-pointed star.

Template patterns

● **Describe shapes and patterns**

You need:

●●● 2 identical 2-D shapes

●●● tape ●●● scissors

●●● paper ●●● colouring materials

Make one of these templates.

a Tape two identical shapes along touching sides like A. Or along partially touching sides like B.

b Draw round the outline of your template. Now draw more outlines and try to make them fit together.

c Use coloured pencils to decorate your pattern.

A 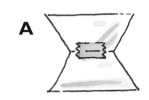 **B**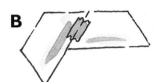

Make a template like this.

a Draw round a plastic square. Cut out the square shape.

b Cut a semi-circle from one side. Slide it to the opposite side and tape it in place.

c Now cut out a triangle from one of the other sides. Slide it across the shape and tape it in place.

d Draw round the outline of your template several times to make a pattern with the outlines fitting together. Use coloured pencils to decorate your pattern.

  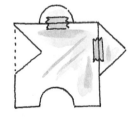

What if your template is a regular hexagon?

Paper folding

● **Create shapes using folding and cutting**

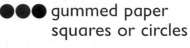
You need:

●●● gummed paper
squares or circles

●●● scissors

●●● ruler

1 Fold your square into quarters each time.

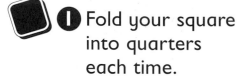

2 Make these patterns by folding and cutting.
Mark the lines of symmetry with a pen.
Stick the patterns in your exercise book.

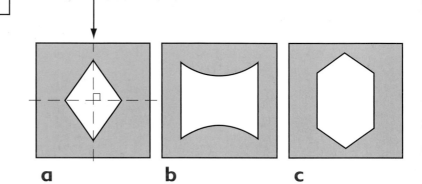

         a   **b**   **c**

1 Fold the square or circle into quarters each time.

2 Find ways to make these patterns.
Mark the lines of symmetry with a pen.
Stick the patterns in your exercise book.

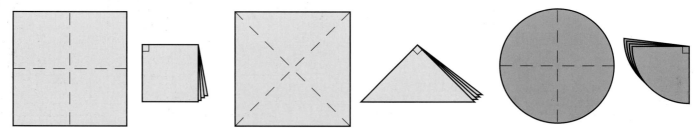

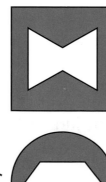

Design two more patterns of your own.
Mark the lines of symmetry and stick them into your exercise book.

Line up the litres

● **Read scales to the nearest division or half division**

Look at the levels of orange juice in jugs **a** to **g**.
Read the scale to the nearest half litre.
Write down how much juice there is in each jug.

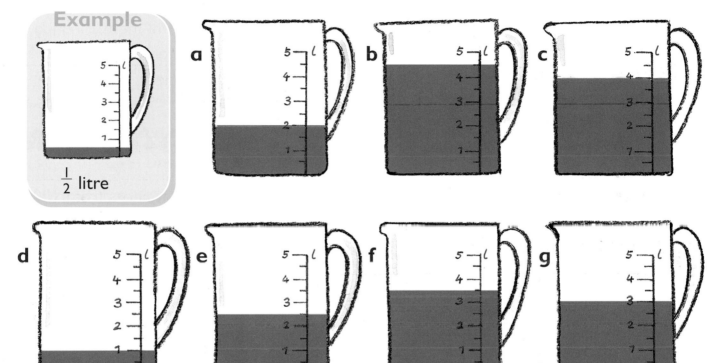

Example

$\frac{1}{2}$ litre

a **b** **c** **d** **e** **f** **g**

❶ Look at the jugs in the ■ section.
Write down how much orange juice there is in each
jug in millilitres to the nearest $\frac{1}{2}$ litre.

❷ You have to refill the jugs to the 5 litre mark. Write
down how much juice you will add to each jug.

Look at the jugs in the ■ section.

❶ Work out how much juice you used altogether to
refill jugs **a** to **g** to the 5 litre mark.

❷ The orange juice from which two jugs combined together is:

a 5 litres?   **b** 6 litres?   **c** 7 litres?   **d** 8 litres?

Example

500 ml

How much does it hold?

Copy this table into your exercise book.

Container	Estimate in ml	Measure in ml

You need:

- ● containers from 100 ml to 500 ml
- ● 500 ml measuring jug
- ● water
- ● funnel

Work with a partner.

❶ Find different containers.

Estimate how much each will hold, to the nearest 100 ml.

Write your estimate in the second column.

❷ Measure each container using a measuring jug.

Write the amount in the third column.

You need:

- ●● containers from 100 ml to 1000 ml
- ●● 1 litre measuring jug
- ●● water
- ●● funnel

Work in a small group.

❶ Find different containers. Estimate how much each will hold, to the nearest 100 ml. Write your estimate in the second column.

❷ Measure each container using a measuring jug. Write the amount in the third column.

Find the difference in millilitres between different pairs of containers.

Writing capacities

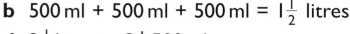
Know how many millilitres are the same as one litre

1 Read these statements. Write down the statements which are true.

a 1 litre = 1000 ml

b 500 ml + 500 ml + 500 ml = $1\frac{1}{2}$ litres

c 400 ml + 200 ml = $\frac{1}{2}$ litre

d $3\frac{1}{2}$ litres = 3 l 500 ml

e $\frac{1}{2}$ litre = 500 ml

200 ml

f You can fill three glasses with this bottle of orange.

2 Write 3 true statements of your own.

500 ml

1 Choose and write the best estimate of the capacity of each of these.

a	b	c	d

a	b	c	d
100 ml 1000 ml 10 l	100 ml 500 ml 5000 ml	1 l 15 l 50 l	4 l 40 l 400 l

2 Find the capacities to complete these tables.

has the same capacity as

a
1 l 500 ml ⟷ $1\frac{1}{2}$ l
2 l 500 ml ⟷ ☐ l
☐ l ☐ ml ⟷ $5\frac{1}{2}$ l
7 l 500 ml ⟷ ☐
☐ l ☐ ml ⟷ $10\frac{1}{2}$ l

b
$3\frac{1}{2}$ l ⟷ 3 l 500 ml
$4\frac{1}{2}$ l ⟷ ☐ l ☐ ml
☐ l ⟷ 6 l 500 ml
☐ l ⟷ 8 l 500 ml
$9\frac{1}{2}$ l ⟷ ☐ l ☐ ml

Investigate filling litre containers from 1 l to 20 l using these jugs. Make a table to record your findings.

a	b	c	d

1 l   2 l   4 l   8 l

Fireworks pictograms

● **Show information using pictograms and bar charts**

You need:
●● squared paper
●● ruler

① Copy this pictogram. Count each type of coin. Draw a ◯ to stand for two coins and complete the pictogram.

② Coins collected for bonfire night

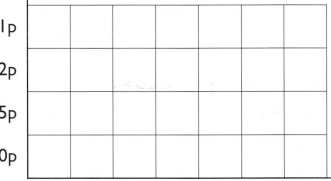

	Number of coins
1p	
2p	
5p	
10p	

Key
◯ stands for 2 coins

② Use the information in your pictogram to answer these questions.

a How many 2p coins were collected?

b How many 5p coins were collected?

c Which is the most common coin?

d Which is the least common coin?

e How many coins were collected altogether?

③ Write a sentence about the information displayed in your pictogram.

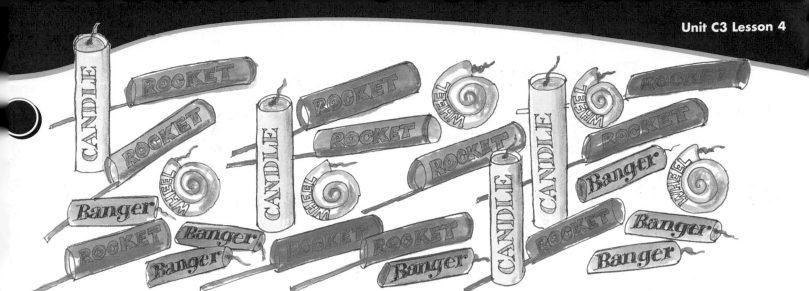

1 Copy this pictogram. Count each kind of firework.
Choose a symbol to stand for two fireworks. Complete the pictogram.

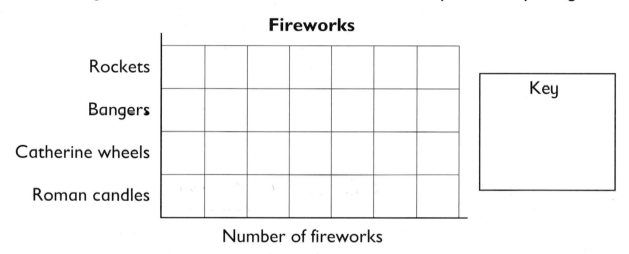

Fireworks

Rockets

Bangers

Catherine wheels

Roman candles

Number of fireworks

Key

2 Use the information in your pictogram to answer these questions.
   a How many Rockets are there?
   b How many Bangers are there?
   c Which is the most common firework?
   d How many more Rockets than Catherine wheels are there?
   e How many fireworks are there altogether?
   f How many fireworks are not Roman candles?

3 Write a sentence about the information displayed
in your pictogram.

 Draw a bar chart for the data in the ● section.

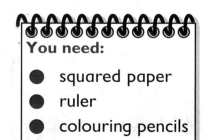
You need:
● squared paper
● ruler
● colouring pencils

33

Pool tables

1 Dana recorded the colours of the balls she potted playing pool.

Pool ball	Tally	Frequency
Red	卌 卌 |||	
Yellow	卌 ||	
Green	卌 卌 卌 卌 ||	
Blue		
Black	|||	

a Copy the tally chart.

b Count the tally marks. Write the totals in the Frequency column.

c Dana potted 17 blue balls. Show this on the chart.

d How many balls did Dana pot altogether?

2 Yuk Ha made a tally chart for the balls he potted.

a Copy his tally chart.

b Draw the tally marks he made.

Pool ball	Tally	Frequency
Red		9
Yellow		20
Green		12
Blue		26
Black		6

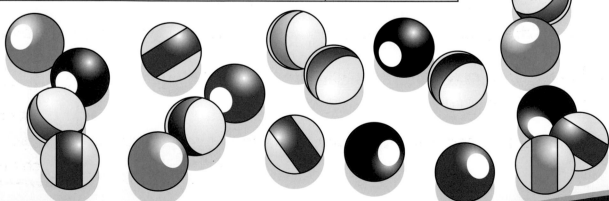

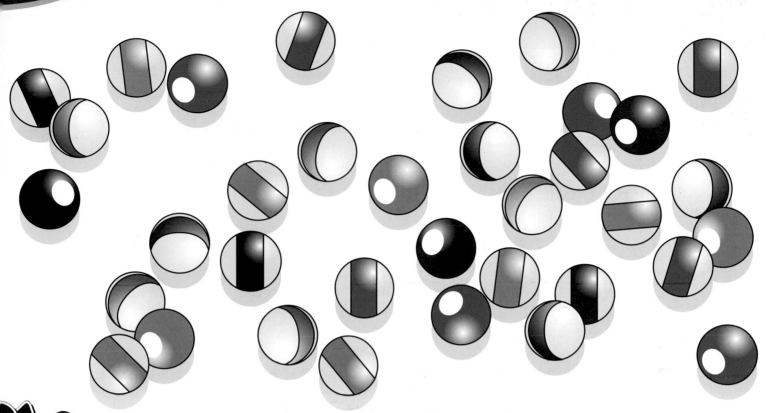

 1 Copy the tally chart. Make a tally mark for each ball on both pages. Calculate the frequencies.

Pool ball	Tally	Frequency
Red		
Yellow		
Green		
Blue		
Black		

2 Now use the information in the table to answer these questions.

a Which ball colour has the highest frequency?

b How many pool balls are there altogether?

c Write your answer to question **b** using tally marks grouped in fives.

3 Write two sentences about the information displayed in your table.

Draw a bar chart for the tally chart in the 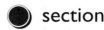 section.

You need:
● squared paper
● ruler
● colouring pencils

Pet bar chart

Work in pairs.

Copy the tally chart.

Roll the dice 50 times. Match the number to the animal. Make a tally mark for each animal. Count the tally marks and write the totals.

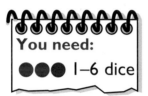
You need:
●●● 1–6 dice

Animal	Tally	Frequency
cat		
dog		
rabbit		
mouse		

1 Copy and complete the bar chart to record the information in the table you completed for the activity.

You need:
- squared paper
- ruler
- colouring pencils

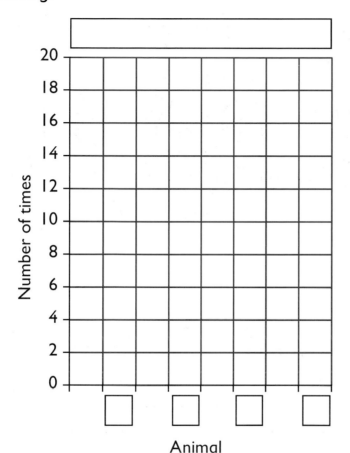

Number of times

Animal

2 Use the information in your bar chart to answer these questions.

a What does the tallest bar show?

b Which animal did you roll least?

c How many times did you roll a dog?

d How many times did you roll a cat?

3 Write two sentences about the information displayed in your bar chart.

 Draw a pictogram for the data in the activity.

You need:
- squared paper
- ruler

Banana bar chart

❶ Copy the table below.

Bananas	Tally	Total
3		
4		
5		
6		
7		

❷ For each person, count the number of bananas eaten and make a tally mark. Then complete the table.

1 Copy and complete the table below using the information from the table in the 📖 section.

Bananas	Frequency
3	
4	
5	
6	
7	

2 Draw a bar chart.

3 Use the information in your bar chart to answer these questions.

a What was the largest number of bananas someone ate?

b How many people ate five or six bananas?

c How many people ate less than four bananas?

4 Write a sentence about the information displayed in your bar chart.

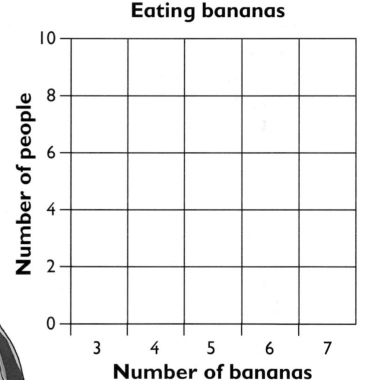

Eating bananas

Number of people (vertical axis: 0, 2, 4, 6, 8, 10)

Number of bananas (horizontal axis: 3, 4, 5, 6, 7)

 Investigate the number of fruits your classmates have eaten in the last five days. Collect the information in a tally chart. Draw a bar chart to show your results. Write two sentences describing your results.

School activities

 The bar chart shows the activities children chose for Sports Day.

1 How many children chose Throwing activities?

2 What was the most popular activity?

3 Copy and complete the pictogram for the data.

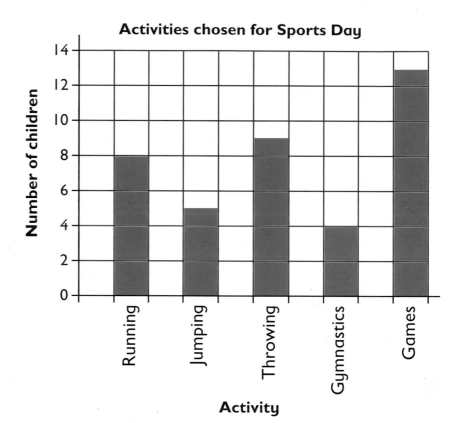

Activities chosen for Sports Day

Activities chosen for Sports Day

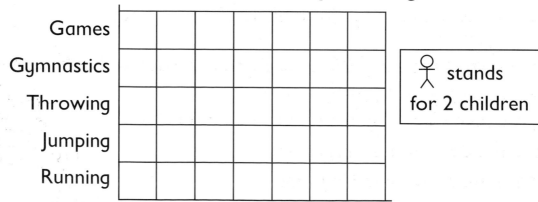

Number of children

stands for 2 children

Work in pairs.

Imagine that the children in your class are going to take part in a photography competition. Each person can submit a photo on any two of these topics:

You need:
- squared paper
- ruler
- colouring pencils

people	animals
buildings	sport
countryside	transport

❶ Each person needs to copy this chart.

Topic	Tally	Frequency
People		
Buildings		
Countryside		
Animals		
Sport		
Transport		

❷ Collect the data from the class and complete the tally chart.

❸ Present your data in a bar chart or pictogram.

❹ Write two sentences describing what you found out.

❶ Make a tally chart using the Sports day activities in the ■ activity.

❷ Ask each person in the class:
'Which activity would you choose for Sports Day?'

❸ Record the data in the tally chart.

❹ Illustrate the data using diagrams.

❺ Compare the results from your class with those in the ■ activity.
Write two sentences.

Fishy Venn diagrams

● **Place objects on a Venn diagram**

1 Copy the Venn diagram.

2 Draw ♡ for each seashell.

3 Count the seashells. Write the totals in the boxes.

4 How many seashells are only red?

5 How many seashells are red and blue?

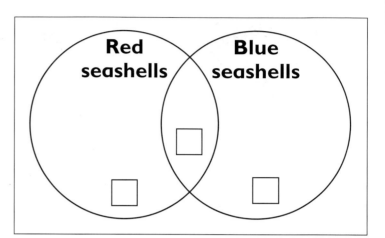

1 Copy the Venn diagram.

2 Draw each fish like this ⋈ • .

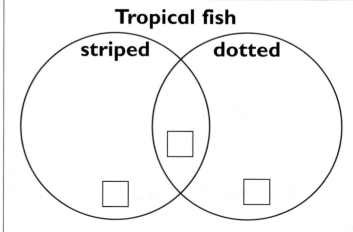

3 Count the fish. Write the totals in the squares.

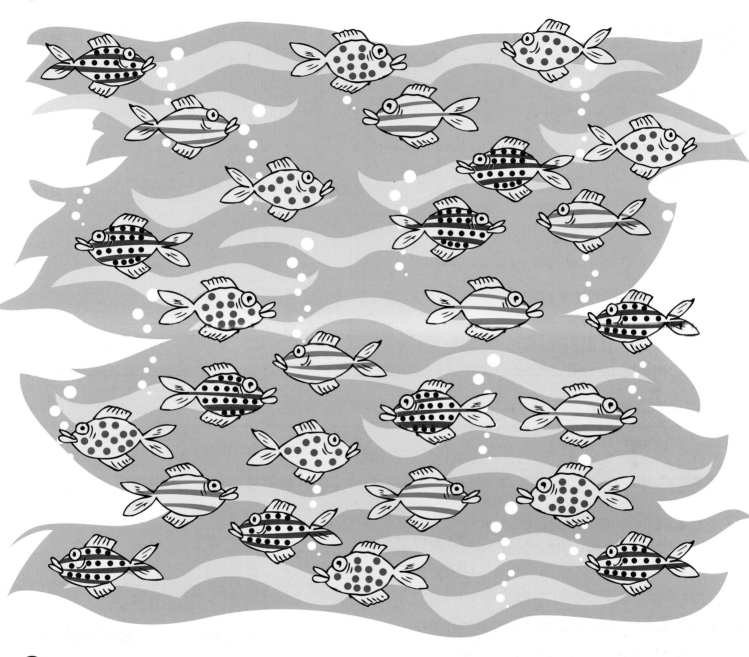

4 How many fish are striped?

5 How many fish are striped and dotted?

6 How many fish are not dotted?

 Sort the fish into striped and green sets.

Shapes Carroll diagrams

● Sort objects using Carroll diagrams

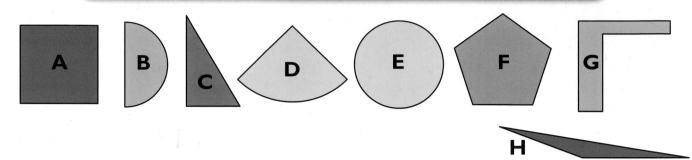

 ① Copy the Carroll diagram.

② Write the letter of each shape in the correct set.

③ How many shapes have curved lines?

④ How many shapes do not have curved lines?

Curved lines	No curved lines

 ① Copy the Carroll diagram.

② Look at the shapes at the top of the page. Write the letter of each shape in the correct set.

③ Count the shapes in each set and write the totals in the circles.

④ How many shapes do not have a right angle?

⑤ How many shapes have symmetry and a right angle?

	Symmetry	No symmetry
Right angle	◯	◯
No right angle	◯	◯

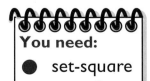

You need:
● set-square

44

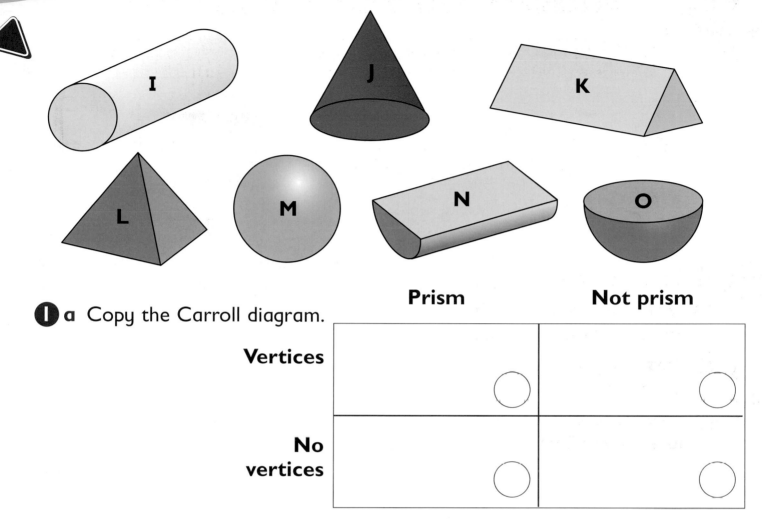

Prism **Not prism**

1 a Copy the Carroll diagram.

	Prism	Not prism
Vertices	◯	◯
No vertices	◯	◯

b Write the letter of each shape in the correct set.

c Count the shapes in each set and write the totals in the circles.

d How many shapes do not have vertices?

e How many shapes have vertices but are not prisms?

2 Sort all the shapes in the ◼ and ◢ sections using this Carroll diagram.

	Flat	Solid
Curved	◯	◯
Not curved	◯	◯

Adding in a different way

● Develop and use written methods for addition

Work out the answer to each calculation. Show your working as set out in the examples below.

a 45 + 32 = ☐   **b** 63 + 36 = ☐

c 54 + 64 = ☐   **d** 75 + 62 = ☐

e 83 + 44 = ☐   **f** 61 + 57 = ☐

g 94 + 76 = ☐   **h** 163 + 35 = ☐

i 147 + 52 = ☐   **j** 136 + 28 = ☐

Example

34 + 55 = 89

30 + 4
50 + 5   +
_____
80 + 9

a 165 + 34 = ☐   **b** 128 + 71 = ☐

c 118 + 64 = ☐   **d** 165 + 47 = ☐

e 107 + 79 = ☐   **f** 146 + 63 = ☐

g 118 + 53 = ☐   **h** 168 + 74 = ☐

i 153 + 127 = ☐   **j** 147 + 154 = ☐

Example

164 + 67 = 231

100 + 60 + 4
     60 + 7   +
_____
100 + 120 + 11

Explain why this method makes adding easier.

Subtracting in a different way

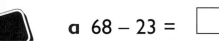
● **Develop and use written methods for subtraction**

Work out the answer to each calculation. Show your working as set out in the examples below.

a 68 – 23 = ☐   **b** 54 – 21 = ☐

c 76 – 32 = ☐   **d** 75 – 43 = ☐

e 61 – 37 = ☐   **f** 86 – 42 = ☐

g 97 – 53 = ☐   **h** 177 – 24 = ☐

i 184 – 53 = ☐   **j** 168 – 45 = ☐

Example

$$67 - 24 = 43$$

$$\begin{array}{r} 60 + 7 \\ 20 + 4 - \\ \hline 40 + 3 \end{array}$$

a 172 – 24 = ☐   **b** 157 – 29 = ☐

c 189 – 34 = ☐   **d** 197 – 51 = ☐

e 182 – 23 = ☐   **f** 196 – 63 = ☐

g 138 – 47 = ☐   **h** 198 – 85 = ☐

i 173 – 39 = ☐   **j** 161 – 44 = ☐

Example

$$167 - 48 = 119$$

$$\begin{array}{r} \overset{50}{} \quad \overset{1}{} \\ 100 + 60 + 7 \\ 40 + 8 - \\ \hline 100 + 10 + 9 \end{array}$$

How would you work out this calculation using the same method? 126 – 57. Explain your working.

182 – 76 = 106

$$100 + \overset{70}{80} + \overset{1}{2}$$
$$70 + 6 -$$
$$\overline{100 + 0 + 6}$$

Doubling and halving

- **Double and halve whole numbers**

Double each of the bus numbers and halve each of the car numbers.

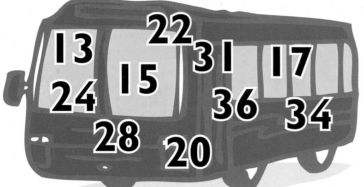

A game for 2 players.

- Take turns to roll the dice and make two two-digit numbers, e.g. 6 and 3 makes 63 and 36. If both of the dice numbers are odd, roll the dice again.

- Double one of the numbers and halve the other, i.e. $63 \times 2 = 126$ and $36 \div 2 = 18$.

- Compare your numbers with your patner then follow the rules to see how many points each player wins for that round.

- The winner is the player with more points after 10 rounds.

A game for 2 players.

- Take turns to roll the dice and make two two-digit numbers, e.g. 5 and 2 makes 52 and 25. If both of the dice numbers are odd, roll the dice again.

- Double one of the numbers and halve the other, i.e. $25 \times 2 = 50$ and $52 \div 2 = 26$.

- Now add both answers together, i.e. $50 + 26 = 76$.

- That is your score for that round.

- The winner of each round is the player with the larger total.

- Play 10 rounds.

You need:
- ●● 2 × 1–6 dice
- ●● pencil and paper

Multiplying and dividing larger numbers

● **Multiply and divide a two-digit number by a one-digit number**

Use the colour code for each of the numbers to answer the calculations.

6   78   4   64   2   83   9   97   7   5   56   49

a ▢ × ▢ = ?   **b** ▢ × ▢ = ?   **c** ▢ × ▢ = ?

d ▢ × ▢ = ?   **e** ▢ × ▢ = ?   **f** ▢ ÷ ▢ = ?

g ▢ ÷ ▢ = ?   **h** ▢ ÷ ▢ = ?   **i** ▢ ÷ ▢ = ?

a ▢ × ▢ = ?   **b** ▢ × ▢ = ?   **c** ▢ × ▢ = ?

d ▢ × ▢ = ?   **e** ▢ × ▢ = ?   **f** ▢ × ▢ = ?

g ▢ ÷ ▢ = ?   **h** ▢ ÷ ▢ = ?   **i** ▢ ÷ ▢ = ?

j ▢ ÷ ▢ = ?   **k** ▢ ÷ ▢ = ?   **l** ▢ ÷ ▢ = ?

a ? × ▢ = 322   **b** ▢ × ? = 512   **c** ? × ▢ = 234

d ▢ × ? = 448   **e** ▢ × ? = 594   **f** ? ÷ ▢ = 13 R3

g ▢ ÷ ? = 27 R2   **h** ? ÷ ▢ = 22 R3   **i** ? ÷ ▢ = 17 R3

Michael and Sophie go to the rugby

● Solve word problems in 'real life' and money, using one or more steps

Use the information to answer each word problem. Show all your working.

The Stadium	Stand	Crowd
	North Stand	642
	South Stand	868
	East Stand	474
	West Stand	285

Merchandise Stall

Programme	£8	Scarf	£6
Sweat shirt	£34	Poster	£12
T-Shirt	£22	Mug	£7
Cap	£4	Umbrella	£15

a Sophie buys 4 programmes. How much does this cost her?

b Mr Avery bought an umbrella, a mug and a cap. How much did he spend?

c How many people are sitting in the North and West Stands altogether?

d Before the match, the stall sold 8 sweat shirts. How much money did it take?

a What is the total cost of a programme, a T-shirt, a poster and a scarf?

b How many people are sitting in the North and South stands altogether?

c Sophie buys 2 caps, a poster and 3 mugs. How much does this cost her?

d How many more people are sitting in the South Stand than in the East Stand?

e Altogether the stall sold 87 caps. How much money did it take on caps?

f A programme seller sold 86 programmes before the match. How much did she take?

a Half the people in the East Stand are club members. How many is this?

b Michael bought 5 T-shirts and 5 scarves. How much was this?

c Altogether the stall sold 96 scarves. How much money did it take on scarves?

d The stall sold 60 umbrellas. How much did it take?

e What is the total number of people in the stadium?

f Altogether the stall sold 786 programmes. How much money did it take?

Mrs MacSporran goes shopping

● **Solve word problems involving capacity**

Mrs MacSporran bought these groceries at her supermarket.

① List the shopping

  a in order of height, smallest first.

  b in order of capacity, least amount first.

② Write what you notice about your two lists.

Look at the list at the bottom of the page.

① Mrs MacSporran bought one of each of these items to get one free.

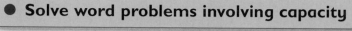

  tomato sauce   olive oil   salad dressing   orange drink

Write down how many millilitres of each item she got altogether.

② She bought two each of these items and got two free.

  shampoo   shower gel   toothpaste

Work out how many millilitres of each item she got altogether.

> If I buy the toothpaste I'll get one free.
> That's 100 ml + 100 ml = 200 ml.
> What a bargain!

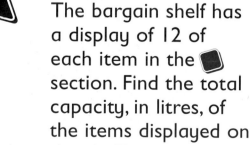

The bargain shelf has a display of 12 of each item in the ▪ section. Find the total capacity, in litres, of the items displayed on the shelf.

Shop 'n' save
Buy 1, get 1 free

tomato sauce	150 ml
olive oil	500 ml
salad dressing	250 ml
orange drink	750 ml
shower gel	300 ml
toothpaste	100 ml
shampoo	400 ml

5 ml measure

● **Solve problems and puzzles involving capacity**

100 ml

Copy and complete.

a 1 spoon holds 5 ml

b 2 spoons hold ☐ ml

c 4 spoons hold ☐ ml

d 5 spoons hold ☐ ml

e 10 spoons hold ☐ ml

f ☐ spoons hold 100 ml

5 ml

A medicine spoon
holds 5 ml

Example

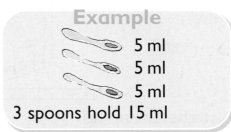

5 ml
5 ml
5 ml
3 spoons hold 15 ml

1 Match these labels to the correct medicine bottle. One spoon holds 5 ml.

a 1 spoon
every day
for 10 days

b 2 spoons
twice a day
for 5 days

c 3 spoons
every day
for 5 days

d 1 spoon
3 times a day
for 10 days

e 2 spoons
twice a day
for 10 days

50 ml

100 ml

150 ml

75 ml

200 ml

2 Here are some labels for the blue bottle of medicine. Copy and complete the table.

400 ml

Spoons	How often each day	Number of days	Amount
1	8	10	400 ml
2	4		400 ml
4		10	
8	1		

Write different labels for a 200 ml bottle of medicine.

Airport times

● **Work out the start or end time for an activity**

The Rossi family is flying to Italy.

To pass the time at the airport Nico makes this table.

Copy and complete Nico's table.

2:15 add on 15 minutes is 2:30

Event	Minutes	Time
Arrive airport		2:15
Queue	15	2:30
Check-in at desk	5	
Snack	25	
Walk to lounge		3:10
Watch aircraft	15	
Read comic	35	
Board plane	10	
Ready for take-off		4:15

① The *Airporter Buses* arrive every ten minutes at these terminals. Copy and complete the times for Services A, B and C.

	Gatwick South	Gatwick North	Heathrow Terminal 4	Heathrow Central
Service A	9:00			
Service B	9:10	9:15		10:20
Service C			10:15	

❷ How long is the bus journey from:

a Gatwick South to Gatwick North?

b Gatwick North to Heathrow Central?

c Gatwick South to Heathrow Terminal 4?

Use the bus times to help you answer these questions.

The Pedianni family is travelling from Gatwick South to Heathrow Central. If they board the bus at 10:50 at Gatwick South, what time will they arrive at Heathrow Central?

Angle allsorts

● Test whether an angle is equal to, bigger than or smaller than a right angle

You need:
●● set-square
●● ruler

1 Check the size of these angles with a set square.

a b c d e f

2 Copy and complete this table.

Less than a right angle	More than a right angle

1 Copy this table.

Less than a right angle	About right angle	More than a right angle

2 Check the size of these kite angles with your set-square.

3 Write each letter in the correct column.

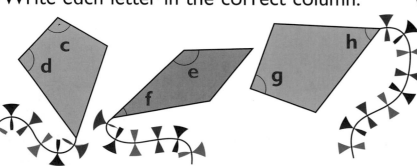

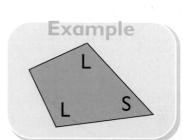

Draw two kites.
Mark the smallest angle with the letter S.
Mark the largest angles with the letter L.

Example

Robot 1, 2, 3

● **Make and describe right-angled turns**

You need:

● 1 cm squared paper
● ruler

A robot began this pattern... then ran out of ink!

Copy this 1, 2, 3 pattern on to squared paper.
Start near the middle of the paper.

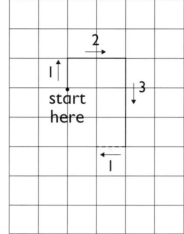

Repeat the pattern
three times starting
where the last pattern
ends each time.

1 Fold the sheet of squared paper in half and mark a starting
dot on each half sheet.

a Copy the robot pattern 1, 4, 2. **b** Copy the robot pattern 2, 4, 1.
Repeat it three times. Repeat it three times.

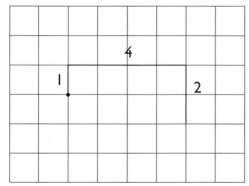

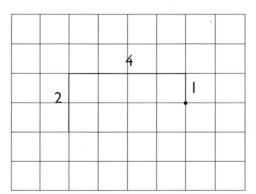

2 Look at your completed patterns.

a Write how the two patterns are the same.
b Write how the two patterns are different.

Make up a pattern of your own.

Splitting numbers

● **Partition numbers in different ways**

 Copy and continue the patterns.

a 62 = 60 + 2
= 50 + 12
= 40 + 22

b 85 = 80 + 5
= 70 + 15
= 60 +

c 99 = 90 + 9
= 80 +
=

Copy and continue the patterns.

a 528 = 500 + 20 + 8
= 400 + 120 + 8
= 300 +

b 749 = 700 + 40 + 9
= 600 + 140 + 9
= 500 +

c 963 = 900 + 60 + 3
= 800 + 160 + 3
=

d 805 = 800 + 0 + 5
= 700 + 100 + 5
=

e 667 = 600 + 67
= 500 + 167
= 400 +
=

f 798 = 700 + 98
= 600 + 198
=

g 361 = 300 + 60 + 1
= 300 + 50 + 11
= 300 +

h 574 = 500 + 70 + 4
= 500 + 60 + 14
=

 Find four different ways of partitioning each of these numbers.

a 2468 **b** 3579

Post code sorting

- **Partition numbers in different ways**
- **Recognise and continue a pattern**

At the Sorting Office, letters are fed into a machine. The machine digitally reads the 2-digit post code and sorts the letter.

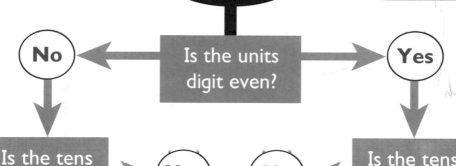

Example

42 → units digit even
   → tens digit even
   → box D

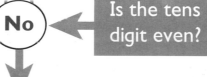

Start

No ← Is the units digit even? → Yes

No ← Is the tens digit even? → Yes   No ← Is the tens digit even? → Yes

A   **B**   **C**   **D**

a Find out in which box, A, B, C or D, each post code number from 10 to 40 belongs by taking it along the branches of the sorting diagram from Start.

b Draw four boxes. Label them A, B, C and D. Record each post code in the correct box.

1 Continue for 2-digit numbers up to 99.

2 Order the numbers in each box by grouping them in 50s, 60s, 70s and so on.

3 Look for patterns and write what you notice.

Design a sorting diagram for 3-digit numbers.

Be an adder

● **Develop and use written methods for addition**

Work out the answers to these calculations.
Add the tens, then the units.

a 52 + 45 = ☐

b 36 + 23 = ☐

c 41 + 27 = ☐

d 24 + 45 = ☐

e 53 + 35 = ☐

f 64 + 38 = ☐

g 27 + 54 = ☐

h 48 + 35 = ☐

i 65 + 29 = ☐

j 66 + 25 = ☐

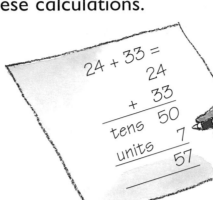

24 + 33 =

```
      24
  +   33
tens  50
units  7
      57
```

Example

24 + 33 = 57

```
       2 4
   +   3 3
tens   5 0
units    7
       5 7
```

Work out the answers to these calculations.
Add the hundreds, then the tens, then the units.

a 136 + 23 = ☐   **f** 165 + 129 = ☐

b 145 + 34 = ☐   **g** 132 + 193 = ☐

c 152 + 45 = ☐   **h** 175 + 144 = ☐

d 127 + 48 = ☐   **i** 159 + 716 = ☐

e 159 + 137 = ☐   **j** 163 + 158 = ☐

Example

136 + 23 = 159

```
             136
    +         23
hundreds     100
   tens       50
  units        9
             159
```

Explain two things you like about this method for addition.

Be a subtracter

● **Develop and use written methods for subtraction**

Work out the answers to these calculations.
Subtract the units and then the tens.

a 67 − 54 = ☐

b 77 − 36 = ☐

c 64 − 37 = ☐

d 65 − 43 = ☐

e 72 − 45 = ☐

f 93 − 34 = ☐

g 85 − 51 = ☐

h 94 − 42 = ☐

i 183 − 65 = ☐

j 151 − 63 = ☐

Example

$$86 − 32 = 54$$

```
   86
 −  2
   84
 − 30
   54
```

Work out the answers to these calculations.
Subtract the units, then the tens, then the hundreds.

a 164 − 42 = ☐

b 184 − 73 = ☐

c 194 − 48 = ☐

d 166 − 73 = ☐

e 148 − 52 = ☐

f 195 − 83 = ☐

g 163 − 39 = ☐

h 242 − 174 = ☐

i 205 − 116 = ☐

j 238 − 94 = ☐

Example

$$275 − 126 = 149$$

```
   275
 −   6
   269
 −  20
   249
 − 100
   149
```

Explain two things you like about this method.

Find the mistake

● **Use written methods for addition and subtraction**

Each of these calculations has a mistake. Find the mistake and write the calculation out correctly.

a 32	b 42	c 34	d 54 – 21	e 68 – 34
26 +	27 +	55	54	68
50	70	90	– 1	– 4
6	9	9	52	64
56	79	99	– 20	– 30
			32	24

1
a 136	b 127	c 173	d 125	e 184
43 +	63 +	21 +	133 +	151 +
100	100	100	200	200
60	80	90	50	130
9	10	5	7	5
169	180	195	257	235

f 146 – 52	g 167 – 59	h 173 – 46	i 292 – 75	j 205 – 63
146	167	173	292	205
– 2	– 9	– 7	– 5	– 3
144	158	166	297	202
– 50	– 50	– 40	– 70	– 60
104	107	126	227	252

2 Make up one addition and one subtraction calculation with hidden mistakes for your friend to find.

Write two top tips – one for addition and one for subtraction – to help someone not to make mistakes.

60

Seaside shopping

● **Solve one-step and two-step problems**

Answer these questions.
Show all your working.

 57p

 86p

 £1.20

❶ Sue buys an ice cream and a windmill. How much does she spend?

❷ Jane has £1. She buys a windmill. How much change does she get?

❸ Evie buys an ice cream. She had £1. How much does she have left now?

❹ George wants to buy a boat and a windmill. How much money will he need?

❺ Max buys a boat and pays with a £2 coin. How much change does he get?

❶ **a** Joshua buys a windmill, an ice cream and a boat. How much does he spend?

  b Joshua pays with a £5 note. How much change does he get?

❷ Sally bought two ice creams and came out of the shop with 20p. How much money did she have before she paid for the ice creams?

❸ Helen bought two boats and a windmill. She paid with a £5 note. How much change did she get?

❶ Nick has £2.43 and then he finds a £2 coin. He goes into the shop and buys two ice creams. How much money has he got left?

❷ Julie buys three of everything. How much does she spend?

Cake fractions

● **Use diagrams to compare fractions**

 Write the number of chocolate cakes.

a 　b 　c 　d 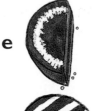　e 　f

 1 Copy the number line. Fill in the missing fractions.

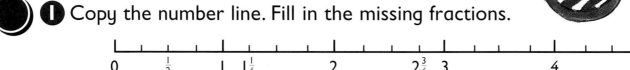

2 For each pair of fractions, write the larger fraction.

a  　b  　c

d  　e  　f

3 Write any number that lies between each of the following.

a 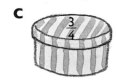 　b

c 　d

Write the number that is halfway between these.

a  　b 　c

d  　e  　f

Estimating fractions

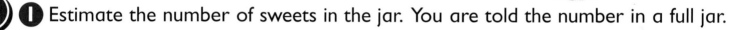
● **Identify and estimate fractions**

Write the fraction of cheese which has been shaded brown.

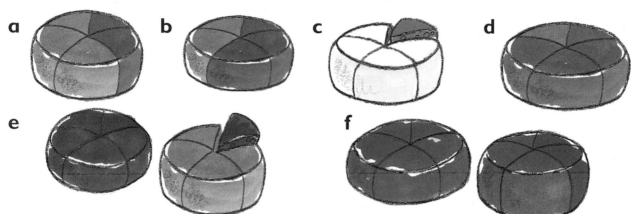

a　　　　**b**　　　　**c**　　　　**d**

e　　　　　　　　　**f**

① Estimate the number of sweets in the jar. You are told the number in a full jar.

a 80　　　**b** 80　　　**c** 100　　　**d** 100

② Estimate the number of sweets in a full jar. You are told the number in the jar.

a 10　　　**b** 8　　　**c** 8　　　**d** 6

① Estimate the fraction of an hour that has passed.

a　　　　**b**　　　　**c**　　　　**d**

   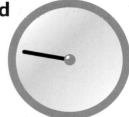

② What time could it be if the hour hand has gone
about two thirds of the way round the clock face?

Fractions of lengths

● **Find unit fractions of numbers and quantities**

 1 Copy and complete this statement.

To find half you need to divide by ☐.

2 Work out half of these lengths. Write the division calculation.

a    b    c    d

24 cm   38 cm   56 cm   72 cm

 1 Estimate half the length of each object.

a    b   c    d

46 cm   98 cm   218 cm   454 cm

2 Estimate a quarter of the length of each object.

a 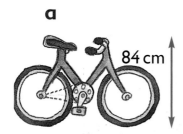   b 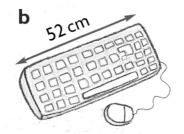   c 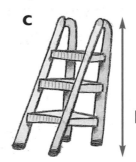   d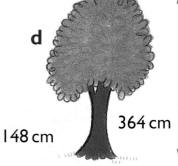

84 cm   52 cm   148 cm   364 cm

 Estimate the length of each object.

a 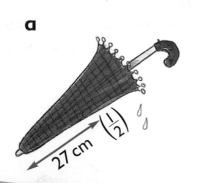   b   c 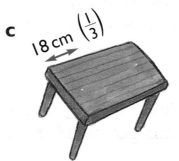   d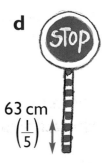

27 cm ($\frac{1}{2}$)   34 cm ($\frac{1}{4}$)   18 cm ($\frac{1}{3}$)   63 cm ($\frac{1}{5}$)

Investigating fractions

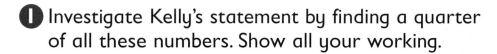

● **Follow a line of enquiry**

Kelly says, 'I tried to find a quarter of the following numbers and only some worked out exactly but I don't know why.'

❶ Investigate Kelly's statement by finding a quarter of all these numbers. Show all your working.

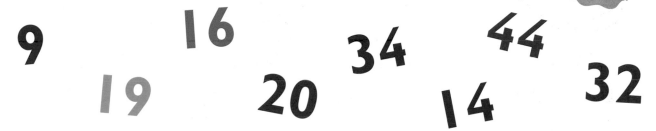

9 **16** **34** **44**

19 **20** **14** **32**

❷ What do you notice about all the numbers that you can find a quarter of?

❸ What would you say to Kelly so she understands why?

Marlow says, 'To find a third of a number and get a whole number answer you must always start with a number that ends in 3.'

❶ Is he right? How will you investigate and prove if he is right or wrong?
Show all your working.

❷ Now you have investigated what Marlow said, what would you say to him?

HINT
Think about how to lay out your working.

When you are investigating a statement, what are the different things you need to remember?

On and back multiples

● **Recognise multiples**

You need:
●●● 1–6 dice
●●● 2 counters

A game for 2 players.

Rules

- Each person places their counter on 1.

- Take turns to roll the dice and move your counter the number of spaces shown on the dice.

- If you land on a multiple of 5, then move *on* to the next multiple of 5.

- If you land on a multiple of 2, then move *back* to the previous multiple of 2.

- If you land on a number that is a multiple of 2 and a multiple of 5, then move *on* to the next number which is a multiple of 5 and a multiple of 2.

1	2	3	4	5	6	7	8	9	10
11	12	13	14	15	16	17	18	19	20
21	22	23	24	25	26	27	28	29	30
31	32	33	34	35	36	37	38	39	40
41	42	43	44	45	46	47	48	49	50
51	52	53	54	55	56	57	58	59	60
61	62	63	64	65	66	67	68	69	70
71	72	73	74	75	76	77	78	79	80
81	82	83	84	85	86	87	88	89	90
91	92	93	94	95	96	97	98	99	100

- The winner is the first person to reach 100.

 Play the game as described in the section, but:

- if you land on a multiple of 3, then move *on* to the next multiple of 3

- if you land on a multiple of 4, then move *back* to the previous multiple of 4

- if you land on a number that is a multiple of 3 and a multiple of 4, then move *on* to the next number which is a multiple of 3 and a multiple of 4.

 Choose your own multiples to move *on* and *back*. For example, move forwards on multiples of 4 and backwards on multiples of 6.

Crack the code

- Know by heart the multiplication facts for the 2, 3, 4, 5, 6 and 10 times tables and the related division facts

Work out the answers to the multiplication and division facts. Then use your answers and the code to work out the answers to the riddles.

A	B	C	D	E	F	G	H	I	J	K	L	M
40	15	2	30	32	27	24	100	6	54	48	4	25

N	O	P	Q	R	S	T	U	V	W	X	Y	Z
3	28	8	16	36	12	7	18	16	10	35	42	20

1. $16 \div 2 =$
2. $5 \times 8 =$
3. $18 \div 3 =$
4. $15 \div 5 =$
5. $28 \div 4 =$
6. $36 \div 6 =$
7. $6 \div 2 =$
8. $4 \times 6 =$
9. $5 \times 3 =$
10. $6 \times 7 =$
11. $30 \div 10 =$
12. $6 \div 3 =$
13. $5 \times 5 =$
14. $3 \times 5 =$
15. $8 \times 4 =$
16. $6 \times 6 =$
17. $2 \times 6 =$

What type of painting do maths teachers most enjoy?

1 2 3 4 5 6 7 8 9 10 11 12 13 14 15 16 17

1. $5 \times 8 =$
2. $3 \times 9 =$
3. $6 \times 6 =$
4. $30 \div 5 =$
5. $8 \times 4 =$
6. $18 \div 6 =$
7. $10 \times 3 =$
8. $7 \times 6 =$
9. $4 \times 7 =$
10. $2 \times 9 =$
11. $12 \div 6 =$
12. $10 \times 4 =$
13. $27 \div 9 =$
14. $14 \div 7 =$
15. $7 \times 4 =$
16. $6 \times 3 =$
17. $24 \div 8 =$
18. $35 \div 5 =$
19. $14 \times 2 =$
20. $12 \div 4 =$

What would you get if you crossed a dog and a calculator?

1 2 3 4 5 6 7 8 9 10 11 12 13 14 15 16 17 18 19 20

A game for 2 players.
- Shuffle the cards and place them face down in a pile.
- Take turns to pick up the top two cards and multiply the two numbers together.
- The winner of the round is the player with the larger product. The winner collects all four cards.
- Continue to pick two cards each, and multiply the two numbers together.
- When all the cards have been used, the winner is the player who has collected more cards.

You need:
- pack of playing cards (picture cards removed)

Multiplying 2-digit numbers

● **Multiply a two-digit number by a one-digit number**

Example

67 × 4

Estimate 70 × 4 = 280

×	60	7
4	240	28

```
   240
 +  28
   268
```

or

```
     67
  ×   4
    240    (60 × 4)
     28    ( 7 × 4)
    268
```

Approximate the answer to each of these calculations. Then use a written method to work out the answers.

a 73 × 4 **b** 82 × 3 **c** 93 × 5 **d** 73 × 4

e 68 × 3 **f** 79 × 5 **g** 84 × 2 **h** 97 × 3

 1 Hit the target using a dart of your choice. Multiply the number on the target by the number on the dart to get your score. Your teacher will tell you how many calculations to make.

 3    6    5    4

 63   86   52   79   47   94   36   88   68   75

2 What is the highest score you can make? Write the calculation.

3 What is the lowest score you can make? Write the calculation.

 What if you used the same darts as in the ■ section and these targets?

 165   142   137   158   194

Your teacher will tell you how many calculations to make.

Dividing 2-digit numbers

● **Divide a two-digit number by a one-digit number**

Approximate the answer to each of these calculations.
Then use a written method to work out the answers.

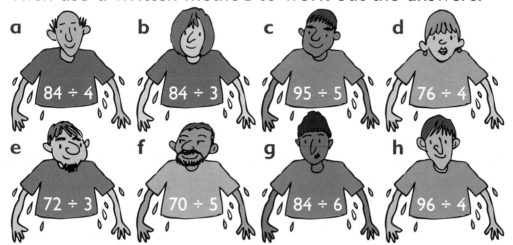

a 84 ÷ 4
b 84 ÷ 3
c 95 ÷ 5
d 76 ÷ 4
e 72 ÷ 3
f 70 ÷ 5
g 84 ÷ 6
h 96 ÷ 4

Example

88 ÷ 3
Estimate
90 ÷ 3 = 30

$$\begin{array}{r} 88 \\ -\ 60 \quad (20 \times 3) \\ \hline 28 \\ -\ 27 \quad (9 \times 3) \\ \hline 1 \\ \hline \end{array}$$

Answer = 29 R1

Hit a teacher using a sponge of your choice. Divide the number on the
teacher by the number on the sponge to get your score. Your teacher will
tell you how many calculations to make.

2   6   3   4   5

77   78   89   70   81
92   83   94   66   95

What if you used the same sponges as in the ● section and these teachers?

186   172   164   158   143

Your teacher will tell you how many calculations to make.

A night at the theatre

- Solve word problems in 'real life' and money

Tickets

Use the information to answer the word problems.

Tickets	
Front Stalls	£46
Rear Stalls	£38
Circle	£42
Balcony	£30

Item	Number in tray	Price
Programme	25	£6
Ice cream	40	£4
Chocolates	12	£8
Bag of sweets	8	£5

a Stan buys two balcony tickets. How much does this cost him?

b Jacob buys one rear stalls ticket and pays with a £50 note. How much change does he receive?

c If Julia sells all the ice creams in her tray, how much money will she take?

d Harold buys two programmes and a bag of sweets and pays with a £20 note. How much change does he receive?

---

a Peter buys two rear stall tickets and pays with four £20 notes. How much change does he receive?

b Julia works out that before the show starts she has taken £84 on programmes. How many programmes has she sold?

c A group of nine friends each buy a circle ticket. How much does this cost them altogether?

d Of the 40 ice creams in Julia's tray, half are chocolate, eight strawberry and the rest vanilla. How many are vanilla?

---

a How much more expensive is it to buy 5 front stall seats than 5 rear stall seats?

b 9 friends each buy a programme. 4 buy an ice cream, 3 buy chocolates and 2 buy sweets. How much does this cost?

c Max bought some circle seats. It cost £210. How many circle seats did he buy?

d If Julia sold everything in her tray, how much money would she take?

e The theatre has a promotion. Buy five or more front stall tickets and receive £5 off each ticket. How much do six front stall tickets cost?

f There are 150 balcony seats. If all the balcony tickets were sold, how much money did the theatre take on balcony seats?

Maths Facts

Problem solving

The seven steps to problem solving

1 Read the problem carefully. **2** What do you have to find?

3 What facts are given? **4** Which of the facts do you need?

5 Make a plan. **6** Carry out your plan to obtain your answer. **7** Check your answer.

Number

Positive and negative numbers

Place value

1000	2000	3000	4000	5000	6000	7000	8000	9000
100	200	300	400	500	600	700	800	900
10	20	30	40	50	60	70	80	90
1	2	3	4	5	6	7	8	9

Number facts

— Multiplication and division facts —

	×1	×2	×3	×4	×5	×6	×7	×8	×9	×10
×1	1	2	3	4	5	6	7	8	9	10
×2	2	4	6	8	10	12	14	16	18	20
×3	3	6	9	12	15	18	21	24	27	30
×4	4	8	12	16	20	24	28	32	36	40
×5	5	10	15	20	25	30	35	40	45	50
×6	6	12	18	24	30	36	42	48	54	60
×7	7	14	21	28	35	42	49	56	63	70
×8	8	16	24	32	40	48	56	64	72	80
×9	9	18	27	36	45	54	63	72	81	90
×10	10	20	30	40	50	60	70	80	90	100

— Fractions and decimals —

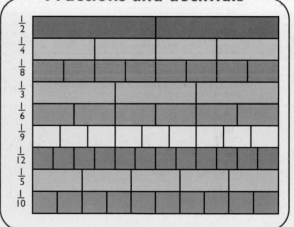

$\frac{1}{2}$ $\frac{1}{4}$ $\frac{1}{8}$ $\frac{1}{3}$ $\frac{1}{6}$ $\frac{1}{9}$ $\frac{1}{12}$ $\frac{1}{5}$ $\frac{1}{10}$

Calculations

— Addition —

Whole numbers

Example: 845 + 758

```
  845            845
+ 758    →     + 758
 1500           1603
   90            ₁₁
   13
 ____
 1603
   ₁
```

Money

Example: £26.48 + £53.75

```
 £26.48          £26.48
+£53.75   →     +£53.75
 70.00          £80.23
  9.00           ₁ ₁ ₁
  1.10
  0.13
 _____
 £80.23
   ₁
```

Calculations

Subtraction

Example: 162 − 115

```
  162                162              50  12                    5 12
−   5              − 115        100 + 60 + 2̶                   1̶6̶2̶
  157                  5 → 120   − 100 + 10 + 5              − 115
−  10                 42 → 162          40 + 7                   47
  147                 47
− 100
   47
```

Multiplication

Example: 82 × 7

Grid method   or   Partitioning

82 × 7 = (80 × 7) + (2 × 7)

= 560 + 14

= 574

```
×    80     2
7   560    14   = 574
```

```
    82              82            82
  ×  7            ×  7          ×  7
   560  (80 × 7)   560           574
    14  ( 2 × 7)    14             1
   574             574
```

Division

Example: 87 ÷ 5

```
87 ÷ 5 = (50 + 37) ÷ 5                 87                  5) 87
       = (50 ÷ 5) + (37 ÷ 5)    or   − 50  (10 × 5)   or    − 50  (10 × 5)
       = 10 + 7 R 2                    37                     37
       = 17 R 2                      − 35  ( 7 × 5)         − 35  ( 7 × 5)
                                       2                      2
                             Answer   17 R 2       Answer   17 R 2
```

Shape and space

2–D shapes

    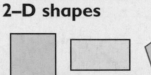

circle | right-angled triangle | equilateral triangle | isosceles triangle | square | rectangle | pentagon | hexagon | heptagon | octagon

3–D shapes

 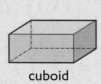

cube | cuboid | cone | cylinder | sphere | triangular prism | triangular-based pyramid (tetrahedron) | square-based pyramid